YAAAWN! STREEETCH! Did you
have a good night's sleep?

3

Everybody needs sleep. You work hard playing and learning every day.

At night your body needs to rest. What happens when you sleep?

Your body
gets more
energy
during sleep.

Your body also repairs itself. Sleep is a time for your body to heal cuts, **bruises** and sore **muscles.**

Your muscles
rest when
you sleep.
But your
brain keeps
working.

Your brain keeps the rest of your body busy. Your heart beats. Your lungs breathe. And your body grows as you sleep.

Your brain also dreams when you sleep. A dream is a story happening in your brain.

You dream every night. You don't remember most of your dreams. You have to wake up at just the right time to remember a dream.

What happens when you don't get
enough sleep? You feel tired when
you get up in the morning.

12

You might be in a bad mood. You might feel clumsy.

Your brain has a hard time working
when you don't get enough sleep.
You cannot **concentrate** as easily.

You might have trouble making
decisions. You might forget things.

You are more likely to be ill if you don't get enough sleep.

It is harder for your body to fight off **diseases.**

Most children need 10 to 12 hours of sleep every night. What can you do to get a good night's sleep?

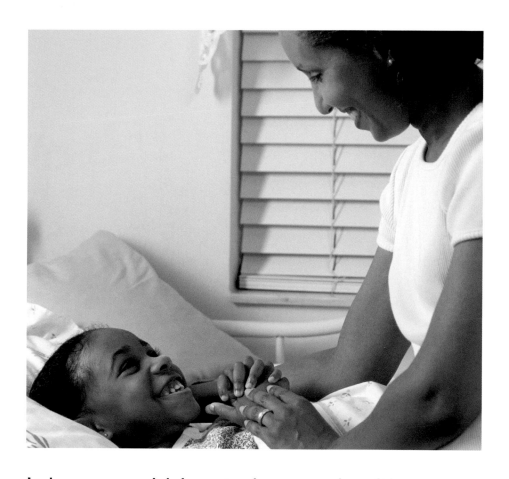

It is a good idea to have a bedtime
routine. Get ready for bed the same
way each night. This will help your
body know when it is time to sleep.

Put your pyjamas on.

Brush your
teeth. Wash
your face.

Read a book.

Try to go to bed at the same time every night. Wake up at the same time each morning.

What else can you do to sleep well? Eating **healthy** foods will help you sleep better. Too much chocolate or fizzy drinks may keep you awake.

Getting **exercise** during the day can also help you sleep.

We all need
to rest so
that we have
energy for
tomorrow.

Sleep keeps us healthy. Sleep helps
us feel good.

Facts about Sleep

■ Yawning is one of the first signs that you are tired. But yawning is also catching. If you see someone else yawn, it might make you yawn too.

■ A bad dream is called a nightmare.

■ Drinking a glass of warm milk before you go to bed can help you to fall asleep.

■ You will spend about one-third of your life sleeping.

■ Giraffes sleep for only 2 hours a day. Animals like bats and snakes sleep more than 18 hours a day. When a snake sleeps, its eyes stay open because it has no eyelids.

Do You Get Enough Sleep?

How do you feel today? Are you grumpy? Full of energy? Fighting to stay awake? The way you feel might have something to do with how much sleep you get.

Keep track of your sleep for one week. Write down what time you go to bed each night and wake up the next morning. Write down how you feel during the day and when you feel sleepy.

Work out how many hours of sleep you get each night. On which days do you have a lot of energy? On which days do you feel tired? How many hours of sleep do you need to feel your best?

If you think you are getting plenty of sleep but still feel tired all the time, talk to an adult. He or she may be able to help you get a better night's sleep.

Books and Websites

Books

Goulding, Silvia. *Sleeping Well* (Healthy Kids) Cherrytree Books, 2006.

Pipe, Jim. *How Long Did I Sleep?* (How? What? Why?) Franklin Watts, 2003.

Royston, Angela. *Get Some Rest!* (Look After Yourself) Heinemann, 2003.

Websites

Sleep for Kids – Teaching Kids the Importance of Sleep
http://www.sleepforkids.org/

CBBC Newsround Sleep Quiz
http://news.bbc.co.uk/cbbcnews/hi/quiz/newsid_1822000/1822533.stm

Glossary

bruises: dark marks under your skin that appear when you fall over or are hit by something

concentrate: to pay attention or focus on something

diseases: illnesses

energy: power within your body that lets it move and be active

exercise: moving your body so that your muscles keep or increase their strength

healthy: something that helps you stay in good condition or being in good condition physically and mentally

muscles: parts of your body that can make it move

routine: a regular way of doing something

Index

Photo Acknowledgements

The photographs in this book appear with the permission of : © Jose Luis Pelaez, Inc./CORBIS, cover, p 6; © Ed Bock /CORBIS, p 3; © Jim Cummins/CORBIS, p 4; © Paul Barton/CORBIS, p 5; © Todd Strand/Independent Picture Service, p 7; © age fotostock/SuperStock, pp 8, 10, 11, 14, 18, 12, 22, 28; © JLP/Sylvia Torres/CORBIS, p 9; © Ariel Skelley/CORBIS, pp 13, 25; © Michael S Yamashita/CORBIS, p 15; © BananaStock/SuperStock, p 16; © LWA-Stephen Welstead/CORBIS, p 17; © SuperStock, Inc./SuperStock, p 19; © John Henley/CORBIS, p 20; Digital Vision Royalty Free, p 21; © Ken Lax/Photo Researchers, Inc., p. 23; © Royalty-Free/CORBIS, p 24; © JLP/Jose L. Pelaez/CORBIS, p 26; © Françoise Gervais/CORBIS, p 27.